24.45

Understanding
IRAN
Today

IRAN

Michael Capek

Mitchell Lane
PUBLISHERS
P.O. Box 196
Hockessin, Delaware 19707

Astara
Tabriz
Orumiyeh
Ardebil
Maragheh
Rasht
Mahabad
Gilan
Zanjan
Gorgan
Qazvin
Sari
Emamshahr
Mashhad
Sanandaj
Tehran
Semnan
Hamadan
Qom
Bakhtaran
Arak
Kashan
Ilam
Khorramabad
Dezful
Esfahan
Shahr-e Kord
Yazd
Ahvaz
Yasuj
Zarand
Khorramshahr
Kerman
Abadan
Zahedan
Kharg
Shiraz
Bandar-e Bushehr

Iran

Bandar-e 'Abbas
Bandar-e Lengeh
Geshm
Jask
Chah Bahar

TURKEY

SYRIA

LEBANON

PALESTINE

IRAQ

AFGHANISTAN

ISRAEL

JORDAN

IRAN

SAUDI
ARABIA

Mitchell Lane
PUBLISHERS

Printing   1   2   3   4   5   6   7   8   9

Library of Congress Cataloging-in-Publication Data
Capek, Michael.
 Understanding Iran today / by Michael Capek.
    pages cm. — (A kid's guide to the Middle East)
Includes bibliographical references and index.
ISBN 978-1-61228-647-1 (library bound)
1. Iran—Juvenile literature. I. Title.
DS254.75.C36 2014
955—dc23
                                                              2014013222
eBook ISBN: 9781612286709

PUBLISHER'S NOTE: The fictionalized narrative and photographs used in portions of this book are an aid to comprehension. This narrative is based on the author's extensive research as to what actually occurs in a child's life in Iran. It is subject to interpretation and might not be indicative of every child's life in Iran. It is representative of some children and is based on research the author believes to be accurate. Documentation of such research is contained on pp. 60–61.

The Internet sites referenced herein were active as of the publication date. Due to the fleeting nature of some web sites, we cannot guarantee they will all be active when you are reading this book.

To reflect current usage, we have chosen to use the secular era designations BCE ("before the common era") and CE ("of the common era") instead of the traditional designations BC ("before Christ") and AD (*anno Domini,* "in the year of the Lord").

PBP

CONTENTS

BOLD words in text can be found in the Glossary

Introduction

Salaam! [suh-LAHM] This is a word you'll hear often if you travel in the Middle East. The word means "peace," and in Iran it also means "Hello!"

It's easy to find Iran on a map. Do you see the country shaped like a cat leaping over the Persian Gulf? That's Iran! It's big, about 636,000 square miles (1,648,000 square kilometers), the second-largest nation in the Middle East. Iran is surrounded by 10 nations and large bodies of water. It's touched in the north by Azerbaijan, Armenia, Turkmenistan, and the Caspian Sea. To the east are Pakistan and Afghanistan. To the south are

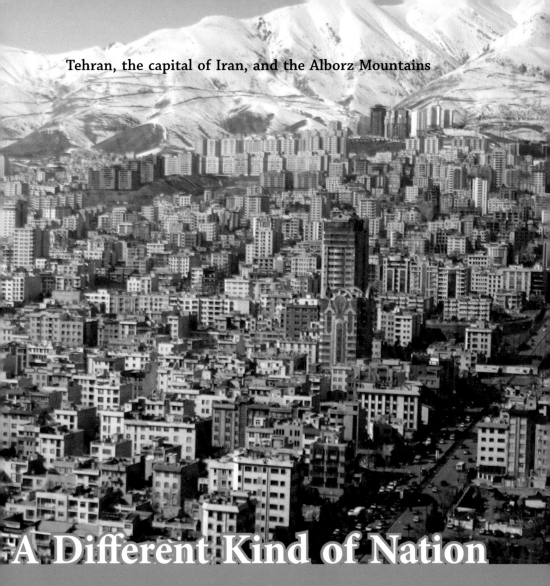

Tehran, the capital of Iran, and the Alborz Mountains

A Different Kind of Nation

the Persian Gulf and the Gulf of Oman. Turkey and Iraq lie to Iran's west.

Iran is very different from its neighbors. For one thing, it's the only nation in the Middle East where people speak Persian rather than Arabic. And that's just for starters!

Best of all, few people anywhere are as eager and happy to share their unusual culture with visitors. When Iranians wish you "Salaam!" they mean it. The land that was once called Persia is as rich and colorful as a Persian carpet. So climb aboard! Any rug in Iran can be a magic carpet to adventure.

Classmates pose for a picture outside the Masjed-e Shāh Mosque in Isfahan, Iran.

CHAPTER 1
A Day with Shirin

It's Muharram, the month of sorrow, so the 300 girls in the schoolyard don't shout or laugh. "It's 7:30!" the principal calls sharply over a loudspeaker. Shirin hurries to join her sixth-grade classmates. Her younger sister, Yara, gets in line with the other second graders.

Shirin's brother is in fourth grade. His school is down the street. Boys and girls go to separate schools in Iran. In fact, they lead separate lives when they are away from home.

Shirin is glad to be wearing the school uniform today. Pale green pants, long-sleeved brown jacket, and large headscarf feel good on a cool morning. Only her face and hands are uncovered. Usually the headscarf, called a *hijab* [HEE-job], is white. But the girls are wearing black during this month of mourning.

Since 1979, Iran has been an Islamic republic. That means people can vote for the president and other government officials. But Islamic **clerics** run the country and make all the important decisions. Long ago, they decided that when girls turn 9, they must cover themselves whenever they leave their homes. They must also observe all Islamic practices. This includes praying each day, memorizing as much of the Quran [kyoo-RAHN, the holy book of the religion of Islam] as they can, and several other things.

In Iran, religion is a big part of every school day. Each teacher leads the girls in saying verses from the Quran. The first graders recite first, then second, third, fourth, and fifth graders.

Iranian schoolgirls prepare to pray. When a Muslim girl reaches age 9, she is expected wear the *hijab* and cover her body except for her face and hands. According to the Islamic tradition, when a girl reaches puberty, she becomes a woman and must start saying daily prayers and going to mosque on Fridays. Shiite schools hold a special program called Jashn-e Taklif, or the Responsibility Celebration. This festival is a special day for Muslim schoolgirls because it marks their passage into adulthood.

The girls repeat their verses loudly. It's important to show great feeling for their religion.

The sixth-grade girls are last. They've learned more verses by heart than the other grades. Shirin knows more than anyone else in her class. She loves reading and saying the verses in Arabic, the language of the Quran. Her own Persian language is prettier, she thinks. But Arabic is the language of the Prophet Muhammad, the founder of Islam. That makes it worth learning.

Someday she would like to become a teacher of the Islamic religion. Perhaps even a cleric. Women clerics help other women understand Islam and the Quran better. There are special schools in Iran that train women to become clerics. Iranian women have many more opportunities now than they did in the past.

When everyone has finished reciting, the teachers give a signal. Shirin and her classmates yell, "Come, Mahdi!" Mahdi is the name of the Twelfth Imam, an important figure in the Shiite branch of Islam. Shiites believe his return will signal the beginning of the end of human life on earth.

The teacher smiles at Shirin, pleased with her enthusiasm. She nods and waves. The girls turn in perfect order and march like soldiers into the school building.

Inside their classroom, the girls remove their *hijabs* and hang them on the backs of their chairs. If a man or boy comes into the room, they'll have to put them back on quickly.

Shirin goes to school every day from Saturday to Thursday. Each school day lasts eight hours. The first subject is history. Shirin has a test on the Islamic Revolution of 1979. The class has been studying this important event for the past month. She's nervous, as she is before every test. It's important for her to do well. Only the top students get to go on to high school and then university.

The first question asks, "Why did the Iranian people rise up against Muhammad Reza Shah?" Shirin writes that the Shah

IN CASE YOU WERE WONDERING

Why is Muharram a month of sorrow in Iran?

In the Shiite form of Islam, the Prophet Muhammad's grandson, Hussein, was killed in battle on the 10th day of Muharram in 680. Shiites observe that terrible event, which they call Ashura, as a day of great sadness. Many people wear black or dark clothing throughout the whole month.[1]

IN CASE YOU WERE WONDERING

Are all Iranian women required to wear head coverings in public places?
After the Islamic Revolution of 1979, all women had to wear a **chador**, or
be arrested. Clothing rules now are not as strict as they once were.[2] In big
cities, most girls and women wear a **manteau** (a loose-fitting coat), and a
hijab.

was untrue to Islam. He loved wealth more than God. He also
let foreign countries take control of Iran. She writes for five
minutes before moving on to the next question.

There are 20 questions in all. When she's done, she feels
satisfied. But she won't be happy until she gets her grade at
the end of the day.

In mid-morning, Shirin and her classmates have a short
break. They go outside and walk around in the schoolyard. But
they can't run or play. They may eat a snack and talk quietly.
Then they have to go back inside for more lessons. During her
science, math, religion, and Arabic classes, Shirin mostly listens
to the teachers and writes in her notebook. Students are rarely
expected to talk. They may raise their hands and ask questions,
but not often. Shirin's parents pay one of her teachers to tutor
her after school three times a week. During that time, they talk
together about lessons and Shirin has the opportunity to ask
as many questions as she wants.

At the end of the day, Shirin learns that she got 18 of 20 of
the questions correct on her history test. That's not good
enough. Her history teacher is also her tutor. They'll discuss the
questions she missed when they meet tomorrow after school.

When school is over, Shirin walks home with her sister and
some of their friends. Her brother walks home with his friends.

Usually she'd watch TV for an hour or two. But today, she
doesn't let herself do that. She starts on her homework. She
usually has two to three hours of extra work each night.[3]

FUN AND GAMES

Even though school is hard, kids in Iran still find time for fun. They love computer games of all kinds. But the most popular game is football (what we call soccer). Nearly everybody plays it. There are some school teams, but mostly kids play soccer in the streets and parks. Girls and boys are usually allowed to play together until girls turn 9. Then they only play with other girls in places where boys aren't around. The same is true of swimming. Iranians love to swim. But girls can only swim at beaches and pools away from public view. Anyone who breaks this rule may be arrested.[4]

Iranians play chess and backgammon, too. Both games were invented in Persia long ago. It's common to see people of all ages playing these games in parks and playgrounds all over the country.

An increasingly popular game is kabaddi, a rough form of tag or catchers. Two teams face each other on a court divided by a center line. One team sends a "raider" to the other side. The raider must keep saying "Kabaddi, kabaddi, kabaddi," without taking a breath. All the while the raider tries to tag the other players out. The team that tags out all of the players on the other side first, wins.

Shih Pin Ju of Taiwan tries to cross the line as players from Iran defend during the women's kabaddi group A round 1 match at the 16th Asian Games in Guangzhou, China, on November 22, 2010. Iran won 62–18.

The Persian leopard is one of the rarest species of animals in Iran. It is believed that 65 percent of the wild Persian leopards in western Asia live in Iran. Illegal hunting and habitat reduction have made it difficult for the big cats to survive. Still, about 550–850 leopards hunt the plains and valleys of Iran.

CHAPTER 2
Land and Animals

Jamal stoops to look at some marks in the hot, dry sand. He's 13, on summer holiday from school. He's seen wavy lines like these before. They were made by a large snake, probably a viper. The wind has not blown down the ridges, so the marks are fairly new. Almost certainly the snake is nearby.

Jamal is in the Naibandan Wildlife Refuge at the edge of the Kavir Desert in central Iran. His father is a scientist and a teacher at Tehran University. His mother is a wildlife photographer. She and Jamal's father are working on a book about Iran's rare wildlife. They especially hope to get pictures of a Persian leopard and an Asian cheetah. Jamal is helping them look for tracks that might lead to animals they can photograph.

The swirling marks lead to a pile of loose rocks. Jamal's parents don't have to tell him to move back. Jamal knows vipers are large and dangerous. Their bite can easily kill a human.

Jamal's mother and father carefully move the rocks and find the snake. It's a desert horned viper. With a special stick, Jamal's father moves the reptile out into the open. His mother snaps pictures of it from all angles.

Jamal has been all over Iran on trips with his parents like this one. He's seen first-hand how beautiful and varied the wildlife and geography of his country is.

Iran is basically a central plateau surrounded by mountains. This wide, flat area is actually made up of three moving **tectonic** plates. These are sheets of rock, deep beneath the ground, that grind and slide against each other. As a result, Iran gets a lot of earthquakes. Some have been severe. A quake near the town of Ferdows, in central Iran, killed 20,000 people in 1968.[1]

Jamal is especially fascinated by mountains. There are four main mountain ranges in Iran. The Salalan and Talesh Ranges are in the northwest **provinces**. The Zagros Mountains stretch 930 miles (1,500 kilometers) from Turkey to the Persian Gulf. The Alborz Mountains lie along the Caspian Sea. Mt. Damavand, the highest peak in the Middle East, is in this range. It towers 18,406 feet (5,610 meters).

Iran's deserts are just as interesting. East of the Zagros Mountains, in the central plateau are two vast deserts, the Kavir and the Lut. The Lut is one of the hottest places on earth, with ground temperatures reaching nearly 160° F (71° C).[2] Part of the Lut is known as "Scorched Wheat." During the 1950s, a load of wheat was abandoned for several days. When it was recovered, the grains had been scorched by the intense heat.

Finding water in these arid regions is rare, though they are dotted by oases. An oasis is a green and fertile place with all sorts of trees, from date palms to pomegranate trees. Villages built in oases grow fields of cucumbers, melons, and other crops that feed millions.

Jamal and his parents stop at a water hole to cool off. As Jamal leans down to splash water on his face, he sees a paw mark in the mud. A cheetah was here not long ago. His mother

IN CASE YOU WERE WONDERING

What large rivers and lakes are in Iran?

Iran's longest river is the Karun River (about 545 miles, or 880 km), which flows from the Zagros Mountains to the Persian Gulf. The largest lake is Urima, a great salt lake in Iran's northeast. The water is too salty for anything to live in, except tiny, almost invisible worms. These worms attract thousands of pink flamingos every spring.

In the oasis village of Yazd, Iran, camels are a common sight, as they have been for centuries. Nearly every home in Yazd is like this one, made of sunbaked mud.

takes pictures of the track. But it is the cheetah itself she really wants to photograph.

Once there were thousands of Asian cheetahs in Iran. Persian princes trained them to hunt gazelles and other game. The spotted cats are the fastest mammals in the world. They reach speeds of 60 miles per hour (96 kilometers per hour). Sadly, less than a hundred are left today, most of them in Naibandan. The chances of seeing one of these beautiful animals are slim.[3]

Iran is home to other amazing wildlife. Gazelles, several types of wild sheep, bears, wolves, and hundreds of different kinds of birds live in the country. Like the cheetah, many are endangered.

Part of the problem is Iran's natural resources—oil and natural gas. They're the most important part of Iran's economy.

> ### IN CASE YOU WERE WONDERING
>
> *Do many Iranians live in air-conditioned houses?*
> Some do, but it's very expensive. In some parts of the country, houses are
> built with badgirs, or wind catchers, on top. These high towers catch cool
> air and send it below. When there is no wind, hot air below moves upward
> and out through the towers.

But extracting them and getting them to consumers is messy
and creates pollution, both air and water. Tehran, Iran's capital
city, has some of the worst air pollution in the world.[4]

Water pollution is also a problem. In the Persian Gulf, oil
tankers constantly come and go. Spills and leaks happen all the
time. The gooey sludge harms sea creatures, such as dolphins
and whales.

The Caspian Sea on Iran's northern border is in trouble, too.
Pollution from the many countries that share the water
endangers plants and animals. The Caspian sturgeon is in
particular trouble. The eggs this fish lays make up 95 percent of
the world's supply of **caviar**. The loss of this costly and (some
say) delicious food worries many people around the world.

Too much hunting and fishing are problems for endangered
species, too. The government of Iran gives out a million hunting
licenses each year and even supplies free bullets to hunters.[4]
Millions of trees are cut each year, for building materials and to
clear land for housing and farming. The loss of these trees
removes important habitat for many of Iran's special creatures.

Jamal and his parents see more cheetah tracks, but no
cheetahs. His mother gets some great photographs of birds,
lizards, and wild boars, though. She even manages to take
some pictures of the cute and funny jerboa. These long-eared
mammals hop on long hind legs like tiny kangaroos, reaching
speeds of 15 miles an hour (25 kilometers per hour).

QANATS

Qanats (kuh-NAHTS) are underground tunnels that carry water in Iran's dry regions. There are more than 20,000 of them, still carrying water today even though many were constructed more than 2,000 years ago. Incredibly, until the late 20th century, qanats supplied 75 percent of the water used in Iran, for both irrigation and household purposes.[5]

Most of the area that qanats irrigate is arid and rainless. Without these channels, farming, and even living in those regions would be impossible.

This network of underground passages was built entirely by hand. Construction began with digging a series of deep holes. Workers went down these holes and dug tunnels outward to springs and streams. They made the tunnels sloped, so the water would run downhill. The water flows along the underground tunnels, some of which are five miles long, to cities or towns. Since the water flows deep underground where it's much cooler than it is aboveground, not much of it evaporates. Bugs, dirt, and other things don't fall into the water as much, either.

This qanat in Fin is from a spring called "The Spring of Solomon," and is thought to be thousands of years old. It is also thought to have been feeding the Sialk area since ancient times.

An Iranian carpet exporter shows a carpet to a customer at his shop in Tehran's old bazaar. Nearly five million Iranians work in the carpet industry today. It's Iran's second-largest industry. Only oil makes more money.

CHAPTER 3
Many Peoples, One Nation

Naveed works in his uncle's carpet shop in Esfahan, Iran's third-largest city. He's 14 and comes to the shop after school three afternoons each week. His uncle and his parents want him to learn the business so he can take over one day.

Lifting and moving heavy, dusty carpets is hard work. Naveed does it because his family needs the money he earns. But it is interesting work, too. Most days, he can't think of any other place he'd rather be.

The Great Bazaar of Esfahan is an endless treasure house, dating back to the seventeenth century. It's a huge marketplace filled with everything a person could ever want to buy. Though Naveed can't afford to buy anything now, it's fun to look at and work near so many beautiful things.

Carpet weaving is as old as Persia itself. Carpets mean much more than just floor coverings to Iranians. They're also used for worship, special gifts, and daily home use. Iranians eat and rest on fancy carpets. So people come here every day searching for just the right color, size, and style. His Uncle Baraz likes to say, "Owning a Persian carpet is like owning a fine horse. Both will increase in value as they get older, if they're loved and treated properly."[1]

Baraz's store has aisle after aisle of carpets from all over Iran, hanging on racks or piled in stacks. Shafts of sunlight slant down from the high arched roof, like golden arrows. Each ray falls on a patch of color.

The carpets are like a map of Iran. In one aisle are orange and gray snowflake designs made by the Lurs in western Iran.

In another are Kurdish rugs, woven in the west, with brilliant reds against black backgrounds. Baluchi carpets on a far rack show the browns and golds of their eastern desert homes. Next to them are Bakhtiari tribal patterns, huge yellow flowers arranged along green vines. On and on it goes. All the various peoples of Iran are here in these stacks and racks of carpets.[2]

Iran itself is a giant Persian carpet. Many different groups are like threads, woven together into a splendid, colorful pattern.

Iran's total population is just over 80 million. Of that number, about 60 percent are Persians. These are people from the ancient Elamite and Aryan tribes that settled in Iran in ancient times. Naveed and other Persian-Iranians are proud of their rich tradition of language and art.

A Persian carpet is woven from other threads, too. Other notable groups in Iran include Azeris, Kurds, Arabs, Lurs, Turkmen, and Baluchis.

Azeris make up about 16 percent of Iran's population. Many are farmers in the northwestern provinces. They speak a mixture of Turkish and Persian.

An estimated 8 million Kurds also live in Iran. A fiercely proud people, they mostly live in the northwest of the country next to Kurdish areas of Iraq and Turkey. Kurds are probably the oldest Iranian people, relatives of the ancient Medes.

IN CASE YOU WERE WONDERING

How big are Persian carpets?

Persian carpets are made in all shapes and sizes. Some are small, such as prayer rugs about 3 feet (1 meter) by 4 feet (1.3 m). Muslims kneel on these during daily prayers. The largest known carpet, woven in Iran in 2007, was made for a huge mosque in the United Arab Emirates. At 60,546 square feet (5,625 square meters), it is about the size of a soccer field. It took more than 1000 workers a year and a half to make it by hand.[3]

Kurds are one of the largest groups of people in the world without their own country. They have often fought for the right to form their own nation. No nation, including Iran, has allowed them to do that.

Arabs in Iran are called *Bandari*. This word means "port," where many Arabs live and work. The Persian Gulf city of Bandar Abbas and nearby islands is home for many Arabs in the Iranian oil industry. Arabs are different from other Iranians in several ways. They speak Arabic instead of Persian, and most are Sunni Muslims. Arab women often wear the *chador*, too, and a full face covering in public. Many Arab men wear a long, flowing robe, sandals, and a long headscarf called a *gutra*.[4]

A Kurdish family in Kermansha, Iran. Kurdish women wear traditional colors and patterns. Once, most Kurds were nomads and lived in tents much of the year. Now, most live in towns and villages, and only a few still follow the old ways.

The Lurs live mostly in the mountainous province of Lorestan in central Iran. They were once mainly a nomadic people. Some Iranian rulers tried to force them to live in cities. But many still hold onto their wandering, herding way of life.

Turkmen look much different from many Iranians. This is because their ancestors came from Mongolia and the Caucasus Mountains in the north. Turkmen have their own dress, too. Even though they're Muslims like most Iranians, their women wear long dresses of bright colors and flowery patterns. They once lived in rugged tents, called *yurts*, like their ancestors. Today, they still raise sheep and goats and live in villages in the northeast near the border of Turkmenistan.

Baluchis are part of a cultural group in southeastern Iran. They live in a region that stretches across the border into Afghanistan and Pakistan. Some Baluchis are still nomads, but most have settled in villages. They are known for their brilliantly colored embroidery patterns and clothing. In Baluchi culture, guests are considered a blessing. It's said that even if a Baluchi's worst enemy comes to his home, that person will be treated as an honored guest.[5]

Many other smaller groups and tribes also call Iran home. Each has its own particular dress, traditions, and customs. It is this rich mix of so many different peoples that makes Iran such a fascinating country.

IN CASE YOU WERE WONDERING

What other craft or art form is Iran known for?

Wood artists in Iran have created some of the most detailed and beautiful marquetry ever made. Marquetry is a method of fine woodworking in which very thin pieces of wood, metal, animal bone, shell, or mother-of-pearl are cut into many different shapes. These pieces are then attached to the flat surfaces of furniture, game boards, boxes, picture frames, and many other things.[6]

THE SPRING CARPET OF KING KHOSROW I

In 531, Khosrow I became king of Persia. To show his wealth and power, Khosrow filled his palace at Ctesiphon with all the luxury of Persia. The room where he met his subjects and other rulers was huge. The arched ceiling was 121 feet (37 meters) high. Ornaments made of jewels and gold were everywhere.

Most amazing was the magnificent carpet that covered the floor. It was 90 feet (27 meters) square, made of the finest silk mixed with threads of gold and silver. The pattern depicted a Persian garden in spring. Thousands of pearls and jewels made up the flowers, water, stalks, and vines. The carpet was meant to show that the king was so powerful he could even make blossoms in the dead of winter.

But there was one natural force that King Khosrow could not control. He died in 579. About 60 years later, invading Arab Islamic warriors captured Ctesiphon and took everything from the palace to become ornaments for mosques and palaces. The magnificent Spring Carpet was taken to Mecca and cut into many pieces.

Only word pictures remain to describe its glory. But the memory of King Khosrow's Spring Carpet became the pattern for all future Persian carpets. Even today, weavers still try to match its beauty.[7]

Most of the brilliant colors in Persian carpets come from natural dyes, such as vegetables, fruit skins, insects, and shellfish.

Relief of Darius in Persepolis. The city of Persepolis was built to show the power and glory of Persian kings. This stone carving shows the king seated on his throne, ready to receive gifts from visitors. Kings and nobles came from all over the Persian Empire to greet and honor the king each year.

CHAPTER 4
The Persian Empire

In 540 BCE, Cyrus II and his army stood before the walls of Babylon. Once it had been the greatest city in the ancient world. Now its people huddled inside, awaiting their fate. Their cruel ruler and his mighty army were gone, defeated in battle. The warriors who defeated them were waiting outside to claim their prize. What would Cyrus do to them and their city?

According to stories, this king was a different sort of warrior king. He followed an old religion called Zoroastrianism. Ahura Mazda, the god he worshipped, was kind and forgiving. In the same way, Cyrus was said to be kind to those who bowed down before him. Stories said he also respected the traditions and customs of those he conquered. Following this code, he had defeated the powerful Medes and Elamites. Now here he was, waiting at the gates of Babylon. The people trembled and wondered. Should they welcome him or fight him to the death to defend their city?

They chose not to fight. When the immense gates opened, Cyrus walked inside. A pathway of flowers and sweet-smelling leaves led him to the beautiful palace. All along the way, the people bowed low. When their new king paused, the people kissed his feet. When they saw his kind face, they knew they had done the right thing. As he took his throne, they sang songs thanking him for bringing the light of freedom and justice to Babylon.[1]

Conquering powerful Babylon was an incredible feat. But Cyrus the Great—as he is known today—was not finished fighting. Yet everywhere he went, he was merciful and generous, loved by those he ruled. He became known as "the father of the Persian people," and is even mentioned in the Bible as "the instrument of God on earth."[2] The empire he created was larger than ancient Egypt, Assyria, or Babylon.

The land that would someday be known as Iran had been settled for thousands of years before Cyrus arrived. The first inhabitants of Iran lived in the Zagros Mountains, perhaps as early as 100,000 BCE. They were nomadic tribes that hunted and gathered there. About 10,000 BCE, they began to settle on the Iranian plateau. The Elamites were probably the first true culture in Iran. About 1500 BCE they lived in Susa (also called Shush), a city in the lowlands along the modern-day border between Iraq and Iran.

The Medes and various Aryan tribes came into Iran around 800 BCE. They fought with the Assyrians and Babylonians for control of cities and resources. In 559 BCE, Cyrus became king and soon began his period of conquest. He died in 530 BCE and was buried in a tomb that still stands today at Pasargadae, his capital city.

The next great Persian king was Darius (duh-RYE-us), who ruled from 522 to 486 BCE. Darius took all previous traditions and languages and formed them into a single Persian culture. He expanded the empire east to India and north to the Danube River in Europe. He also built the magnificent city of Persepolis, which boasted of richly decorated golden palaces and other beautiful buildings. Its gates were made of solid gold and Darius's great meeting hall could hold 10,000 people. People came to Persepolis from all over Persia for parties and festivals. The size and glory of the city proved to all who came how great the king of Persia was.

Darius's empire also had many paved roads, the world's first postal system, and a huge navy. Still, his army was beaten by the Greeks at the Battle of Marathon in 490 BCE. Darius's son Xerxes (ZURK-sees), who succeeded him, was defeated by the Greeks a decade later. While these defeats had little effect on the Persian Empire, things were very different with another Greek. Alexander the Great conquered the Persians and destroyed Persepolis around 330 BCE. The ruins of this once-magnificent city eventually vanished beneath the blowing sands.[3]

Ruins of Persepolis

IN CASE YOU WERE WONDERING

Is Persepolis still in existence?
The ruins of Persepolis were lost until the 1930s. Covered by wind-blown sand, massive staircases and broken columns had to be dug out. The ruins give a good idea of what this magnificent city looked like. Stone carvings along stairways show the pomp and ceremony the city was built for.

When Alexander died in 323 BCE, his empire was divided among his generals. The part that contained modern-day Iran was given to the Seleucids. Parthian and Sassanid rulers followed, and during this time Zoroastrianism became the state religion.[4]

Nearly 1,000 years later, Arab warriors arrived and brought the new religion of Islam with them. Most Persians became Muslims, although some still held onto old Zoroastrian customs and rituals. The Persian and Arabic languages mixed and mingled, too. These elements added to the unique Persian culture.

The Safavid line of rulers (1501–1736) made Shiite Islam the state religion. The Safavids were followed by the Qajar dynasty in 1794. This line of mostly weak and greedy kings, called shahs, ruled in Iran until 1925. During this period, Iran's people suffered from poverty and foreign takeovers.

One brief, shining moment was the Constitutional Revolution of 1905. This people's movement forced the shah to accept a constitution. That document limited his powers and gave the people of Iran a freedom they had never known before. The democracy it created was almost immediately stamped out by the next shah. But the idea that people could rise up and force kings to change was not forgotten.

World War I nearly destroyed Iran as a nation. Even when it was over, the Soviet Union and Great Britain fought over control of Iran's important oil fields.

In 1921, Reza Khan Pahlavi, an officer of the Iranian army, organized a takeover of the government. Shortly afterward, the Iranian parliament placed him on the throne, as Reza Shah. This began a new Pahlavi dynasty. Iranian's dream of a democracy gave way once again to a **monarchy**.[5]

ZOROASTRIANISM

People of ancient Iran worshipped many gods. One of these was Ahura Mazda. Sometime between 1000 and 1500 BCE, a prophet named Zarathustra (or Zoroaster) began preaching that Ahura Mazda was the only true god. He was the creator of light, man, and the universe. Zoroaster also taught that people should live by a high moral code of good deeds. They would face a final judgment and an afterlife, he added. He also taught that Ahura was a good and merciful god, not an angry, cruel one. Mankind was created to be like him, kind and forgiving.

Zoroaster's ideas were contained in a sacred book called the *Zend-Avesta*. It taught that the world was in a constant state of war between two forces. On the side of light and good was Ahura Mazda, the creator of all things. On the other side were demons and the forces of darkness and evil. They were controlled by Ahriman, the Destroyer.

The religion based on Zoroaster's beliefs spread throughout the region during the time of Cyrus the Great. It became the main one on the Iranian plateau before the Arab conquest introduced Islam. By that time, many of Zoroaster's ideas had become part of Persian culture, and they remain so today.[6]

Carved symbol of Zoroaster in Persepolis

Mohammad Reza Pahlavi began his rule as the Shah of Iran on September 16, 1941. During Mohammad Reza's reign, he tried to modernize his nation and make religion less important. Like rulers before him, the Shah loved luxury and ceremony. He wore rich clothes and spent millions of dollars for his own comfort and enjoyment. These things angered Iranians and led to his overthrow during the Iranian Revolution in 1979.

CHAPTER 5
From Monarchy to Theocracy

On February 1, 1979, five million people jammed the streets of Tehran. All of them were looking up, waiting for a glimpse of a special airplane. Aboard was the Ayatollah Khomeini (eye-uh-TOE-luh koh-MAY-nee). He was a Shiite Muslim imam, and the most popular and powerful man in Iran. For the past 15 years he had been living in exile. Now he was coming home.

When his plane landed, the 78-year-old Ayatollah was helped down the stairs. As he reached the bottom, he slowly knelt and kissed the ground. People all over Iran went wild with joy. The shah was gone. The monarchy was officially over. But exactly what kind of government would replace it? Nobody knew, except Ayatollah Khomeini. He alone would decide Iran's future.[1]

By the latter half of the 20th century, the people of Iran had grown tired of shahs. These rulers had wasted billions of dollars on personal luxuries while their people starved. Iranians wanted something new. Around 1960, a popular leader offered it to them.

His name was Ruhollah Khomeini. He received the title "ayatollah" after years of study at Qom, the spiritual capital of Iran. An ayatollah is simply a leader of the Shiite faith. By 1960, Khomeini had earned the title "grand ayatollah." He became the leader of all Shiites in Iran.[2]

After Reza Shah died in 1944, his son Mohammad Reza Pahlavi ascended to the Peacock Throne, the name given to a copy of a gold-and-jewel-covered throne on which Muslim rulers had sat for centuries. According to some estimates, it was worth $13 billion. To the people of Iran, the throne stood for kings who lived and ruled only for their own benefit and pleasure.

Mohammad Reza Pahlavi was even more wasteful and proud than his father. During his reign, he spent huge sums of public money on public spectacles that made him look more grand and kingly. He said his plan was to bring Iran into the modern world. So he outlawed veils for women in public places and took powers away from Shiite leaders.

Iran's people grew more and more angry. They wanted a leader who was both deeply religious and democratic. Their shah was neither of those things. Angry protests against the shah swept through Tehran. Many of these demonstrations were organized by Ayatollah Khomeini and other Muslim leaders. The shah, they preached, had declared war on Islam. It was up to the people to revolt. Riots and protests spread all over the country.

In 1964, the shah ordered Ayatollah Khomeini to leave Iran. It made no difference. The Ayatollah still ran the revolution. By the late 1970s, it seemed clear that the Shah was finished. Ill with cancer and in danger from angry mobs, he left Iran early in 1979. The people went wild with happiness. Some even broke into the palace to take jewels from the Peacock Throne. After all, didn't they belong to the people who had paid for them?

Khomeini returned to joyous celebrations. Almost immediately he was named *faqih*, supreme religious and political leader of Iran for life. Nothing in the country could happen without his permission as Leader of the Revolution.[3]

Joy turned to worry when millions of Iranians learned the Ayatollah's plans. Almost immediately, he set up a government based strictly on Islamic law. The nation was now the Islamic Republic of Iran. It was a **theocracy**.

As soon as he had total control, the Ayatollah arrested all those who had opposed him in the past. Thousands were put in prison and hundreds were killed "as enemies of Islam." Public hangings and beheadings happened almost every day. Laws were passed forcing women and girls to wear the chador in public. Anything Western, particularly American, was outlawed. Any sign of protest against the government was met with extreme violence. Some people began to wonder if life in the Ayatollah's theocracy was any better than life in the shah's monarchy had been.

Ayatollah Ruhollah Khomeini (right) with his son Ahmad Khomeini (center) and Mohammad-Ali Rajai, second president of Iran. Ahmad was one of his father's most trusted advisors and supporters. Rajai was a favorite of the Ayatollah too. But he was officially only president for less than a month before he was assassinated in 1981.

But the Supreme Leader of the Islamic Revolution was in firm control. He tried to get Shiites in other nations to join in a war against America and other non-Muslim countries. Many nations protested. Iran's neighbor Iraq even declared war. Saddam Hussein, Iraq's president, feared the Shiite takeover in Iran. He worried that the revolution might spread to his own nation. He decided to attack first before Khomeini had a chance to attack him. Also, Iran was rich in oil, and the Khuzestan oil fields were right next to Iraq's border. The war, which nobody won, raged from 1980 to 1988.

During that time, many countries cut ties with Iran and imposed **sanctions**. They stopped buying Iran's oil and other products. In many ways, Iran became an isolated, outcast nation in the eyes of the wider world.

Through it all, Ayatollah Khomeini never changed his mind nor his message. He continued to preach his beliefs until he died in 1989.

Ayatollah Ali Khamenei was president of Iran in 1989. But he resigned to become Leader of the Revolution after Ayatollah Khomeini died. Akbar Hashemi Rafsanjani became Iran's president. After Khomeini's death, Iran's constitution was changed, giving the president much more power. Using these

IN CASE YOU WERE WONDERING

What are sanctions?
Sanctions are a type of penalty that one nation imposes on another. For instance, soon after the 1979 Revolution the United States and other nations agreed to stop buying things Iran needed to sell—mainly oil. That action hurt Iran's economy. At the same time, these countries refused to sell certain items, such as medicine, to Iran. The sanctions continued into the 21st century in an effort to force Iran to stop trying to make an atomic bomb. In 2014, Iran agreed to limit its nuclear program, and the US removed some sanctions.

powers, Rafsanjani tried to reconnect Iran to the world through trade and political means. But Khamenei and other Islamic clerics wanted Iran to remain America's enemy, no matter what. Rafsanjani was not able to ease the crippling sanctions the United States and other countries had in place. Iran's economy and its people continued to suffer from shortages of food, medicine, and many other important things. Since then, nearly every president of Iran has faced the same problems.[4]

At the beginning of the 21st century, though, a different issue came between Iran and the rest of the world. For years it had been known that Iran was experimenting with nuclear power. It was suspected that nuclear scientists there were also trying to build an atomic bomb. The idea of an atomic weapon in the hands of an unsteady government made the rest of the world very nervous. The US and Israel were especially worried. Iran's leaders repeatedly said they would like to wipe Israel off the face of the earth. America has long been Israel's best friend and protector. So attacks on Israel could be regarded as attacks on the US.

Iran continued to say it only wanted nuclear power to create better and cheaper electricity. But the country's leaders never let anyone from the outside see what they were really doing.

Things began to change in the past few years. Iran's newest president, Hassan Rohani, was elected in 2013. He reached out to the US and other world powers. He said he would allow inspectors to come into Iran to see that they are not working on atomic weapons. He also said he wanted to reconnect Iran with America and the rest of the world. Rohani said he especially wanted to take steps to end sanctions. The first step was to end any question about whether or not Iran was trying to build an atomic bomb. President Barak Obama answered that the US

Hassan Rouhani (right) became Iran's seventh President in 2013. He is seen here with former president Akbar Hashemi-Rafsanjani at Iran's parliament. One of Rouhani's first acts as president was to phone US President Barack Obama. It was the first time the leaders of the two countries had spoken to each other since 1979.

would be happy to work with Iran, if they really wanted to be friends with America again.[5]

Of course, the final word on anything in Iran still belonged to Supreme Leader Ayatollah Ali Khamenei. Still, the possibility of better relations between Iran's government and America seemed brighter than it had for many years.

THE IRAN HOSTAGE CRISIS

When the Shah left Iran in 1979, he was very sick with cancer. American President Jimmy Carter agreed to allow him to enter a hospital in New York in October. Iran demanded his return but Carter refused.

Several weeks later, hundreds of young Iranians broke into the US Embassy in Tehran and seized more than 60 American personnel. The Revolution was still new and exciting. Iranians were thrilled to be getting the best of "The Great Satan," Khomeini's term for the US. He said the hostages would only be released if America returned the Shah to stand trial and billions of dollars he had supposedly taken from the Iranian people.

Carter refused. Though a few hostages were released, 52 remained in captivity. In April, 1980, Carter ordered a secret, high-risk military operation to free the hostages. Though American aircraft and troops landed in Iran, the mission failed. Eight American servicemen died. It was a huge embarrassment.

The two sides began negotiations, but they dragged on for months. The situation became a major factor in the 1980 presidential election and helped elect Ronald Reagan. The hostages were released moments after Reagan's inauguration in January, 1981. They had been prisoners for 444 days.[6]

Americans were often taken outside and shown to crowds during the hostage crisis. Blindfolds and tied hands were meant to illustrate how powerless the prisoners and America were.

The Imam Reza shrine in Mashhad, Iran, is the largest mosque in the world. It contains the tomb of Imam Reza as well as the Goharshad Mosque, a museum, a library, a cemetery, prayer halls, four seminaries, the Razavi University of Islamic Sciences, a dining hall for pilgrims, seven courtyards with fourteen minarets and three fountains, and other buildings.

CHAPTER 6
A Religion of Joy and Sadness

Pilgrims from all over the country and beyond fill the streets of Mashhad in northeastern Iran. Shirin is here with her cousin, Omid, and some of their friends. They've come on a special bus with hundreds of others to visit the Haram-e Razavi, the tomb of Reza, the Eighth Imam.

Mashhad, Iran's second-largest city and its holiest, is aglow in the cool afternoon sunlight. It's a magical city within a city. All around are golden domes, blue-tiled archways, and spurting fountains. Everywhere strangers greet one another with cries of "Ramadan Mubarak!" ("Ramadan blessings!") To be in Mashhad at this time of year is thrilling. Shirin can barely contain her excitement.

After evening prayers at the Gohar Shad Mosque, it's time to visit Reza's tomb. This is something Shirin has dreamed of since she was small. It's dark now. The domes and glittering towers are lit by a million bulbs. Omid grasps Shirin's hand so she won't get lost in the surging crowd. At the entrance of the Haram, though, he has to let her go. Men and women must enter the tomb area by different doors. Shirin gathers her chador around her, and pushes inside through a door hung with rich carpets. After a while, Omid finds her and they move into the Holy Shrine itself.

Everyone stands looking through a golden grid at the holy tomb of Imam Reza. People of all ages weep openly. Many murmur prayers. Some sway back and forth, moaning. Reza's death was a tragic one, after all. He was murdered in 818. Shirin is quickly caught up in the spirit of the place. She leans against

Omid and cries quietly for a few moments. She whispers a request to the Imam for his help on her exams at the end of the school year.

Crowds moving into the room sweep them apart. Shirin finds Omid waiting in the outer courtyard. He is wiping tears from his eyes, yet beaming with joy. Shirin understands more now what it means to be a Shiite.[1]

Almost everybody (about 98 percent) in Iran today is Muslim. Nearly 90 percent are Shiites [SHEE-ites] and the rest are Sunnis [SOO-nees]. Understanding the difference between these two branches seems hard for non-Muslims, but it's similar to the difference between Protestants and Catholics. Both of these groups are Christians, but each practices the religion differently.[2]

Sunnis and Shiites share many Islamic beliefs and traditions. The most basic are known as the Five Pillars of Islam. All Muslims are required to observe them. The first is to constantly affirm one's belief by saying "There is no god but God (Allah) and Muhammad is his messenger." Next is praying five times each day, both inwardly and also physically by kneeling and bowing, then touching one's head to the ground. Fasting during the month of Ramadan and giving to the poor are two other pillars. The final one is the hajj—a pilgrimage to Mecca, Islam's holiest city.[3]

Like Sunnis, Shiites follow these rules closely, but with several differences. To the statement of their belief, for instance, they add "and Ali is the executor of God's will." Most Shiites also

IN CASE YOU WERE WONDERING

Are people of other religions welcome in Iran?

There are small numbers of Christians and Zoroastrians in Iran. Also, Iran is home to more Jews than any other country in the Middle East except Israel. Each of these groups is allowed to worship freely. They're even permitted to elect one person to speak for them in the parliament.[4]

Muslim Friday mass prayer in Imam Mosque in Isfahan, Iran. The mosque was built during the Safavid Period, between 1501 to 1722. This is the time when Shiite Islam became the main religion of Iran. The mosque has been restored and is considered one of the masterpieces of Persian architecture.

pray only three times during the day. But there is one much more important issue that has divided the two groups for centuries. This has to do with the question of the faith's leadership.

Shiites think that only direct relatives of the Prophet Muhammad can be leaders. Sunnis believe any Muslim who is well-educated and religious can be appointed to lead Muslims in the faith.[5]

The problem for Shiites began long ago. They believe that the Prophet Muhammad meant for his son-in-law Ali to become leader, or caliph, after him. When Muhammad died, a series of three other men became caliph instead. Ali was finally selected as caliph in 656. But he was savagely murdered in 661 during the month of Ramadan. A man named Muawiyah became caliph.

In 680, Ali's son Hussein fought against Yazid I, who had succeeded Muawiyah as caliph. Hussein and other members of Ali's family died in the Battle of Karbala (in today's Iraq) on the 10th day of the month of Muharram.[6]

Today, all Muslims celebrate the month of Ramadan as the joyous month when Muhammad received his message from the angel Gabriel, as recorded in the Quran. But only Shiites mourn for Ali during three days of Ramadan. They also mourn during the 10th day of Muharram, known as the Day of Ashura. After Mecca, Hussein's tomb at Karbala is the Shiites' holiest site.[7]

Over the centuries, Shiites have continued to cling to the belief that only members of Muhammad's family can be imams. These are a group of twelve special men whom Shiites believe were sent by God from 680 to 873 to lead them. The Twelfth Imam, Muhammad al-Muntazar, will reappear one day, Shiites say. He is the Mahdi, or Messiah, who will bring about the end of the world and the Last Judgment. Until then, Shiites believe, all twelve Imams remain in spirit, active and interested in the world. They're always here to help and encourage the faithful to understand God's will and answer prayers.[8]

IN CASE YOU WERE WONDERING

How do Muslims celebrate Ramadan?

Muslims are required to fast between sunrise and sunset every day during the month of Ramadan. This means they do not eat or drink anything. Eid-e Fitr is a feast at the end of Ramadan. Muslims celebrate this happy day in much the same way Christians celebrate Christmas.[9]

THE PROPHET MUHAMMAD

Muhammad was born in Mecca (in modern-day Saudi Arabia) in 570. A successful merchant, he was also very religious. One day in 610, the angel Gabriel appeared to him with important messages from Allah (the Arabic word for God). His purpose in life would be to spread those messages as Allah's prophet on earth. The book containing the messages Muhammad received became the Quran, the holy book of Islam. The words contained in the Quran are the basis of the Islamic faith. Islam means "surrender" or "yield." To be a Muslim means to give up totally to the will of God.

The basic idea that Muhammad preached was that Allah is the one and only God. Many people followed Muhammad's teachings and became Muslims. But during this time, people worshipped many gods. So many of those people fought against the new ideas and against Muhammad. Some even wanted to kill him. He and his followers fled from Mecca to Medina for safety. From there, the Prophet and his followers fought back so that what they believed was the true religion could survive. They were successful. By the time Muhammad died in 632, Islam had begun to spread across the Arabian Peninsula. Soon it would spread across the entire Middle East.[10]

Quran

Haft Sin table

CHAPTER 7
Iranian Culture

It's March, the beginning of spring. For weeks, Fatemeh and her family have been getting ready for Nowruz [now-ROOZ], the Iranian New Year. This is the happiest time of the year for Iranians. Fatemeh and her two brothers have helped clean the house and paint wood trim on the outside. They've all gotten new clothes and shoes.

The celebration begins on the spring equinox (between March 19 and 22, depending on the year) and lasts for 13 days. Friends and relatives visit, bringing baskets of spring flowers. Several old customs and rituals take place. In one of them, a small fire is built in the yard. Everyone in the family, even the little ones, goes outside and jumps over the fire. Ancient people thought this cleared the body of the sickness and weariness of winter. For Fatemeh, it's fun to do things Persians have done since the time when Cyrus the Great held festivities in ancient Persepolis.

Fatemeh helps her mother set up the Haft Sin table. This is another old tradition. On the table they place a group of seven things beginning with the letter S, as well as a variety of other objects. Each one stands for something the family hopes will continue to be part of their lives in the coming year. For example, an apple stands for the sweetness of life. Flowers mean beauty. A goldfish in a bowl stands for life. Candles represent light and happiness. The Quran, of course, is for their religion.

When the moment of Nowruz gets close, the family gathers around the Haft Sin table for prayers. Then they eat *sabiz polo*

Iranians celebrate ahead of Nowruz, the Iranian New Year, in Tehran, Iran, on March 20, 2014. Nowruz marks the first day of spring and the beginning of the new year on the Iranian calendar.

(rice and vegetables) and *mahi* (fish). Fatemeh's mother eats three hard-boiled eggs, one for each of her children. As the spring equinox nears, TV and radio announcements tell them the exact moment. The family hugs and kisses, and the kids get presents.

On the thirteenth day, Nature Day, the family goes for a picnic. They take a shallow pot of newly grown sprouts of

IN CASE YOU WERE WONDERING

What public holidays are celebrated in Iran?
Iran observes numerous holidays. Fifteen are religious, such as Ashura, Ramadan, and the birthday of the Prophet Muhammad. Most non-religious holidays observe historical events or people. These include Revolution Day (February 11), Oil Nationalization Day (March 20), and Islamic Republic Day (April 12).

wheat or lentils, which have been growing for several weeks. After their picnic, they throw the pot into a lake or river. This is like throwing away the old year, so a new one can begin.[1]

One of the best ways of understanding a country is through its food. Like its people, food in Iran varies widely. It seems that each region and city has its own particular dish or favorite food. Many people say that the best way to appreciate Iranian food is to be invited into an Iranian home. If a person travels much in Iran, the chances of that happening are very good. Iranians love having visitors. It's part of their Persian tradition. They actually think of a guest as a "gift from God." Sharing with others thus becomes almost a religious duty.[2] The cry "Nush-e Jan!" is often heard at feasts. The words mean "food is life." The cry is really a wish that guests will enjoy every mouthful of food to the fullest.

The basic foods of most Iranian meals are *chelow* (rice) and *nun* (bread). Both come in a wide variety of types and forms. Yogurt, feta cheese, and fresh fruit are also served with nearly every meal. *Chelow kebab* is often called "the national dish of Iran."[3] This dish includes pieces of meat (usually lamb) and

Chelow kebab and roasted vegetables

vegetables that are stuck on skewers (long wood or metal rods) and roasted over hot coals or in the oven. It's served sizzling hot on top of sweet or spicy rice. Bread is ripped to pieces and used as scoops or to soak up juice. A drink often served with meals is *doogh*, plain yogurt mixed with water and flavored with lime or lemon juice. It's served with mint, salt, and pepper sprinkled on top.[4]

Breakfast usually consists of cheese, bread and jam, and tea. Iranians love black tea served very hot and very sweet. Teahouses, similar to small neighborhood cafes, are in every city. They're popular meeting places for friends and family. Lunch is eaten in the early afternoon and is the biggest meal of the day. Dinner is eaten late, after 7:30 or 8:00, and often consists of leftovers from lunch. It's more like a before-bedtime snack than a meal.[5]

Movies are one of the most popular forms of entertainment in Iran. The Iranian film industry is world-famous for its thoughtful, well-made movies. Many are shown in America and other western countries. Filmmakers sometimes show the bad things about Iran as well as the good. They may make fun of Iran's leaders. Iran's government is not always pleased about this. Some filmmakers have had to leave the country. Others have been arrested. The government doesn't stop everyone, though, and many excellent movies appear each year. The *Children of Heaven*, about a boy's adventures in Tehran, was nominated for the Academy Award for Best Foreign Language Film in 1998. *The White Balloon* (1995), about being a child in Iran, was another award-winning movie.

Music is popular in Iran. Different peoples in Iran have their own styles of folk music. Persian classical music is mostly slow and mournful, but still very popular. Persian instruments have been played for centuries for this type of music. They include the *nay* (a type of flute), *tombak* (a vase-shaped drum), *tar* (a six-stringed instrument like a guitar), and *santur* (a hammered dulcimer). Iran has its own pop and rock stars, too. The pop group Arian became the first group consisting of both men

The Arian Band performing during a concert at the 23rd Fadjr International Music Festival in Tehran. The nine-member band was the first pop music group allowed to perform for large audiences after the Islamic Revolution of 1979.

and women to be accepted after the Islamic Revolution when their first album was released in 2000. They are still popular. So is a second band called O-Hum. A third, Hypernova, got its start in Tehran but had to move to the US in 2007 because authorities didn't like their music.[6]

Early Muslims believed that painting pictures of people and animals was wrong. But some Persian artists painted these subjects anyway. Painting tiny pictures called *minyaturha* became one of Persia's great art forms. The pictures often were done for books, even the Quran. Today, some of these tiny pictures sell for great sums of money.

Some *minyaturha* were based on poems. Poetry has always been a huge part of Persian life and culture. Poets were much admired by early kings and tribal leaders. Their poems were sung or recited as entertainment, bringing great pleasure to royalty and common people alike. At the end of the tenth century, the Persian poet Ferdowsi wrote an epic poem called the *Shahnameh*, or *The Book of Kings*. It describes 1,000 years of history, legends and fantasy. Iranians love the emotion and music of their poems, ancient and modern. During the Constitution Revolution of 1905, poetry was used by the people to express their anger and determination.[7] Poems from all eras are considered national treasures of Persian culture. Poetry is still often read aloud at small family get-togethers and on special occasions, such as weddings and even funerals.[8]

IN CASE YOU WERE WONDERING

Are any Persian poets well-known outside of Iran?
Perhaps the most famous Persian poet is Omar Khayyám, a mathematician and astronomer born around 1050. He's most famous for his beautiful Rubaiyat, a book consisting of a thousand four-line poems about life, suffering, love, and death.

WEDDING CUSTOMS

Weddings in Iran are fancy affairs, filled with old customs and traditions. The wedding is usually held at the groom's home. When he enters, he first sees the bride's face in a mirror lit by two candles. Food, sweets, a basket of colored eggs, and other items are on a white cloth nearby.

During the wedding, friends of the bride sift sugar on her. The mullah, or cleric, reads the marriage contract aloud. Both families have agreed to the terms long before the service. The bride understands it perfectly. But when the cleric asks if she will sign it, she pretends to disappear. When the mullah asks again, the bride's friends pretend she has left. They say, "She went to gather rosebuds" or "She went to the library." The mullah asks three times before the bride "returns" and agrees to sign the marriage contract. To end the ceremony, the bride's mother removes the bride's shoe and puts out candles with it.

A huge feast follows, which usually includes jeweled rice. This sweet dish is made with green pistachios and red barberries to imitate real emeralds and rubies. There's much singing, dancing and more feasting for hours after the wedding, too.[9]

A band plays while a bride goes to her wedding in a decorated wagon pulled by a camel. This is just one of many traditional wedding customs seen in Iran.

RANGINAK (STUFFED DATES WITH WALNUTS)

Dates, called *rotab* in Iran, may be eaten at any time, and have a special meaning during Ramadan. They are said to be the first food the Prophet Muhammad ate to break his fast. Ranginak is delicious eaten warm or cold. Some people like to drizzle honey on their Ranginak for extra sweetness. Be sure to use fresh dates. The dried (candied) kind won't do.

Ingredients

10–12 fresh dates
10–12 walnut halves
½ cup unsalted butter
½ cup white flour
2–3 tbsps. crushed nuts (unsalted pistachios and almonds are best, but walnuts or pecans can be used too)
¼ tsp. cinnamon
2–3 tbsps. honey (if you like)

Instructions

1. Make a small cut in the top of each date and carefully remove the seed. Ask **an adult** before you use a sharp knife or heat the stove.
2. Crush all the nuts (except the walnut halves) and add the cinnamon. Mix them all together well and set aside.
3. Push a walnut half (or a piece that will fit) inside each date. Arrange the stuffed dates close together, side-by-side on a plate or dish. Make sure the slit edges face up.
4. Melt the butter in a pan on medium heat. Add the flour, stirring it into the butter. Keep cooking and stirring the butter-flour mixture for about 3–4 minutes. Be careful not to overcook it. When it's golden brown and creamy, it's ready.
5. Pour the flour-butter mixture over the stuffed dates. Cover each date and let the mixture run down inside with the walnuts.
6. Sprinkle the crushed nut-cinnamon mixture over the dates. Set aside to cool.

PAPER MARBLING

It's thought that the Chinese invented marbled papers. But Persians became famous for making them as early as the 16th century. European and Asian printers and bookbinders used Persian papers as end sheets for their finest books. Collectors today still pay large sums of money for books made with these marbled papers. You can make your own marbled papers. It's a fun project anybody can do.

Materials

Odorless turpentine

Tubes of oil paints (the kind artists use) of various colors

A shallow pan (plastic or aluminum, larger than 8 ½ x 11 inches)

4–5 small paper or plastic cups

4–5 plastic spoons and forks

Paper (any sort will do, but it's fun to try different colors and textures)

Be sure to get an adult to help you with this project. Turpentine is poison and there will be some fumes, even with the odorless kind. Work in an airy place. Also, oil paint will stain clothes, carpets, furniture, and anything else it touches.

Instructions

1. Fill the pan about ⅔ full of water.
2. Put a dab of paint about the size of the end of your thumb in a cup. Add about a teaspoon of turpentine and mix well with a plastic spoon. Use a different cup and spoon for each color you mix. The more turpentine you use, the less bright the colors will be.
3. Sprinkle a spoonful of the paint mixture onto the water. Because oil and water don't mix, the paint will float on the surface. Drip other colors into the water, if you like. Try two or three different colors, to start.
4. Gently swirl the paint around on the surface with a plastic spoon or fork. Let the colors mix and mingle.
5. Hold a piece of paper with both hands over the water and drop it onto the surface. The paper will slurp up the paint. Make sure all parts of the paper touch the water's surface
6. Lift the wet paper out of the water and lay it on a clean, flat surface to dry. Newspapers work well for this.

Try different colors of paint and paper. Use your finished marbled papers for other crafts, such as scrapbooking, bookmarks, or book covers. Some of your creations will even look great framed, like modern art.

WHAT YOU SHOULD KNOW ABOUT IRAN

Official name: The Islamic Republic of Iran
Size: About 636,000 square miles (slightly larger than Alaska)
Population: About 81 million
Provinces: 31. Tehran Province is the largest with about 12 million people. Ilam Province is smallest with about 557,000 people.
Religions: Islam 98%, Christians, Jews, Zoroastrians and others 2%
Official language: Persian
Head of state: Supreme Leader Ayatollah Khamenei
Head of government: President Hassan Rhomani
Capital city: Tehran (also Iran's largest city with more than 8 million people)
Other major cities: Mashhad (2.8 million), Esfahan (1.8 million), Shiraz (1.5 million), Tabriz (1.5 million)
Bordering Countries: Iraq, Turkey, Armenia, Azerbaijan, Turkmenistan, Afghanistan, Pakistan
Bordering bodies of water: Caspian Sea, Persian Gulf
Mountain ranges: Zagros, Salalan, Talesh, and Alborz
Rivers: Karun (Iran's only river suitable for boats)
Largest lake: Lake Urmia
Highest point: Mount Damavand, 18,406 feet (5,610 meters)
Lowest point: Caspian Sea, 92 feet (28 meters) below sea level
Money: the rial
National anthem: The present anthem was adopted in 1990 after Ayatollah Khomeini died. These are the words:

> *Upwards on the horizon rises the Eastern Sun,*
> *The sight of the true Religion.*
> *Bahman—the brilliance of our Faith.*
> *Your message, O Imam, of independence and freedom*
> *is imprinted on our souls.*
> *O Martyrs! The time of your cries of pain rings in our ears.*
> *Enduring, continuing, eternal,*
> *The Islamic Republic of Iran.*

Flag: Green is the color of Islam, and it also suggests growth. White stands for honesty and peace. Red is for the blood of **martyrs**. The red crest in the center consists of the word "God" in Persian with a sword in the middle. The crest is shaped like a tulip. In Iran, tulips are said to grow from the blood of those who give their lives for their country and religion. Also, written 22 times along the edges of the green and red bands are the Persian words "Allahu Akbar," or "God is great."

TIMELINE

BCE

100,000	Early people live in caves in the Zagros Mountains.
10,000	Tribal groups settle in villages on the Iranian plains.
3,000	Aryan groups and Elamites come into southwestern Iran.
559–30	Cyrus II (the Great) rules all Persia.
522–486	Darius extends Persia's borders and power.
486–465	Xerxes reigns over Persia.
332	Alexander the Great conquers Persia and burns Persepolis.

CE

224	Sassanian dynasty begins.
651	Arab invaders bring Islam to Iran.
1501	The Safavid dynasty makes Shiite the dominant form of Islam.
1795	Tehran becomes Iran's capital.
1905	The Constitutional Movement briefly introduces democracy.
1925	Reza Shah takes power.
1941	Mohammad Reza Shah takes power.
1964	Ayatollah Khomeini is arrested and exiled by the Shah.
1979	The Islamic Revolution forces the Shah to leave Iran; the Ayatollah Khomeini returns and takes power.
1979	The Iran hostage crisis begins in November.
1980	The Iran-Iraq War begins.
1981	The Iran hostage crisis ends.
1988	The Iran-Iraq War ends.
1989	Ayatollah Khomeini dies; Ayatollah Khamenei becomes the Supreme Leader.
2005	Iran's nuclear program leads to sanctions and isolation.
2014	Iran agrees to limits on its nuclear power program; President Barack Obama offers to lift some sanctions.

CHAPTER NOTES

Chapter 1: A Day With Shirin

1. Malihe Maghazei, "Iran," *Teen Life in the Middle East*, ed., Ali Akbar Mahdi (Westport, CT: Greenwood Press, 2003), pp. 19–21.

2. Andrew Burke, Virginia Maxwell, and Lain Shearer, *Iran* (Oakland, CA: Lonely Planet Publications, 2012), p. 340.

3. Jane Howard, *Inside Iran: Women's Lives* (Washington, DC: Mage Publishers, 2002), pp. 79–84.

4. Maghazei, pp. 24–25.

Chapter 2: Land and Animals

1. Andrew Burke, Virginia Maxwell, and Lain Shearer, *Iran* (Oakland, CA: Lonely Planet Publications, 2012), p. 318–319.

2. "Gandom Beryan in Lut Desert - hottest place on Earth," Wondermondo.com. http://www.wondermondo.com/Countries/As/Iran/Kerman/GandomBeryan.htm

3. Eskandar Firouz, *The Complete Fauna of Iran* (New York: I.B. Tauris, 2005), pp. 60–61.

4. Burke, p. 64.

5. Wulff, Hans E., "The Qanats of Iran," *Scientific American*, Vol. 218, No. 4 (April 1968), p. 94.

Chapter 3: Many Peoples, One Nation

1. "Iran," *Encyclopedia of Cultures*, Vol. 2, Melvin and Carol R. Ember, eds. (New York: Macmillan Reference USA. 2001), p. 1073.

2. Sandra Mackey, *The Iranians: Persia, Islam and the Soul of a Nation* (New York: Dutton, 1996), pp. 1–2.

3. "World's Largest Carpet Woven for Worshipers," *National Geographic* (August 1, 2007), http://news.nationalgeographic.com/news/2007/08/070801-iran-picture.html

4. Andrew Burke, Virginia Maxwell, and Lain Shearer, *Iran* (Oakland, CA: Lonely Planet Publications, 2012), pp. 211.

5. Ibid., p. 227.

6. *A Survey of Persian Handicraft: A Pictorial Introduction to the Contemporary Folk Arts and Art Crafts of Modern Iran*, Jay Gluck and Sumi Hiramoto Gluck, eds. (Tehran: Survey of Persian Art, The Bank Melli Iran, 1977), pp. 346, 352–353.

7. Mackey, pp. 33–34, 45–46.

Chapter 4: The Persian Empire

1. Sandra Mackey, *The Iranians: Persia, Islam and the Soul of a Nation* (New York: Dutton, 1996), pp. 21–22.

2. Ibid., p. 23.

3. Elton Daniel, *The History of Iran* (Santa Barbara, CA: Greenwood, 2012), pp. 45–49, 272.

4. *Iran: The Essential Guide to a Country on the Brink. Encyclopedia Britannica* (Hoboken, NJ: John Wiley and Sons, 2006), pp. 53–57.

5. Michael Axworthy, *A History of Iran: Empire of the Mind* (New York: Basic Books, 2008), pp. 218–219.

6. Mackey, pp. 16–17.

Chapter 5: From Monarchy to Theocracy

1. Sandra Mackey, *The Iranians: Persia, Islam and the Soul of a Nation* (New York: Dutton, 1996), pp. 271–272.

CHAPTER NOTES

2. *Iran: The Essential Guide to a Country on the Brink. Encyclopedia Britannica* (Hoboken, NJ: John Wiley and Sons, 2006), pp. 118–119.

3. Elton Daniel, *The History of Iran* (Santa Barbara, CA: Greenwood, 2012), pp. 181–183, 190–192.

4. *Iran: a Country Study, Glenn E. Curtis and Eric Hooglund*, eds. (Washington, DC: Library of Congress, Federal Research Division, 2008), pp. 70–73.

5. Kambiz Foroohar, "Rohani Taps U.S. Educated Minister to End Iran Sanctions," Bloomberg Politics, August 5, 2013. http://www.bloomberg.com/news/2013-08-04/rohani-taps-u-s-educated-foreign-minister-to-end-iran-sanctions.html.

6. Hamid Dabashi, *Iran: A People Interrupted* (New York: The New Press, 2007), pp. 166–167.

Chapter 6: Religion of Joy and Sadness

1. Sandra Mackey, *The Iranians: Persia, Islam and the Soul of a Nation* (New York: Dutton, 1996), pp. 107–108.

2. David Waines, *An Introduction to Islam* (New York: Cambridge University Press, 1995), pp. 30–32, 89–93.

3. Vali Nasr, *The Shia Revival* (New York: Norton, 2006), pp. 38–39.

4. Robin Wright, *Dreams and Shadows: The Future of the Middle East* (New York: Penguin Press, 2008), p. 272.

5. Waines, p. 156.

6. Moojan Momen, *An Introduction to Shi'i Islam* (New Haven, CT: Yale University Press, 1985), p. 30.

7. Waines, pp. 161–162.

8. Mackey, pp. 106–107.

9. Najmieh Khalili Batmanglij, *New Food of Life: Ancient Persian and Modern Iranian Cooking and Ceremonies* (Washington, DC: Mage Publishers, 1996), pp. 399–400.

10. Albert Hourani, *A History of the Arab Peoples* (New York: Warner Books, 1991), pp. 15–20.

Chapter 7: Food and Holidays

1. Massaumme Price, "Iranian New Year No Ruz," http://www.iranonline.com/festivals/Iranian-new-year/index.html

2. Burke, p. 296.

3. Najmieh Khalili Batmanglij, *New Food of Life: Ancient Persian and Modern Iranian Cooking and Ceremonies* (Washington, DC: Mage Publishers, 1996), p. 16.

4. Jila Dana-Haeri and Shahrzad Ghorashian, *New Persian Cooking* (New York: I.B. Tauris, 2001), p. 193.

5. Andrew Burke, Virginia Maxwell, and Lain Shearer, *Iran* (Oakland, CA: Lonely Planet Publications, 2012), pp. 296–298.

6. Burke, pp. 315–317.

7. Hamid Dabashi, *Iran: A People Interrupted* (New York: New Press, 2007), pp. 16–19, 89–90.

8. Batmanglij, pp. 295, 400.

9. Ibid, pp. 293–295.

FURTHER READING

Books

Canini, Mikko (editor). *Iran*. Detroit: Greenhaven Press, 2005.

Climo, Shirley and Robert Florczak. *The Persian Cinderella*. New York: HarperCollins, 1999.

Sheen, Barbara. *Foods of Iran*. New York: Kidhaven Press, 2006.

Somervill, Barbara A. *Iran*. New York: Children's Press, 2012.

Spilsbury, Richard. *Iran*. Chicago: Heinemann Library, 2012.

On the Internet

See how much an American dollar is worth in Iranian rials
    http://www.xe.com

Soar through spectacular 360 degree images of Persepolis
    http://www.360cities.net/image/hadish-palace-persepolis#125.73,-10.40,70.0

See pictures and read information about all aspects of Iran's culture and history
    http://www.art-arena.com/iran.htm

Hear Iran's national anthem
    http://www.nationalanthems.info/ir.htm

Hear classical Persian singers Mohammad Reza Shajarian, Sharam Naziri and others
    http://www.last.fm/music/Mohammad+Reza+Shajarian

Hear a popular Kurdish music group
    http://iranians.kodoom.com/en/kamkars/videos/TQwosSMuQaM/.

Listen to Iranian rock group O-Hum and others
    http://www.last.fm/music

Wander through a wealth of information and pictures.
    http://www.great-iran.com/Great-Iran-Home.htm

Explore Iran
    http://www.iexplore.com/travel-guides/middle-east/iran/overview

Works Consulted

Amjadi, Maryam Ala. "Molding minds and taming times: The concept of games in Iran," *Tehran Times*, January 7, 2012. http://www.tehrantimes.com/life-style/94324-molding-minds-and-taming-times-the-concept-of-games-in-iran

Axworthy, Michael. *A History of Iran*. New York: Basic Books, 2008.

Burke, Andrew, Virginia Maxwell, and Lain Shearer. *Iran*. Oakland, CA: Lonely Planet Publications, 2012.

Curtis, Glenn E. and Eric Hooglund, editors. *Iran: A Country Study*. Washington, DC: Library of Congress, Federal Research Division, 2008.

Dabashi, Hamid. *Iran: A People Interrupted*. New York: New Press, 2007.

Dana-Haeri, Dana with Shahrzad Ghorashian. *New Persian Cooking*. New York: I.B. Tauris. 2001.

FURTHER READING

Daniel, Elton. *The History of Iran*. Santa Barbara, CA: Greenwood, 2012.

Ember, Melvin and Carol R. Ember, editors. *Encyclopedia of Cultures*, Vol.2. New York: Macmillan Reference USA. 2001.

Faramarzi, Mohammad Taghi. *A Travel Guide to Iran*. Tehran: Yassavoli Publications, 2000.

Firouz, Eskandar. *The Complete Fauna of Iran*. New York: I.B. Tauris, 2005.

Foroohar, Kambiz, "Rohani Taps U.S.-Educated Minister to End Iran Sanctions," *Bloomberg Politics*, August 5, 2013. http://www.bloomberg.com/news/2013-08-04/rohani-taps-u-s-educated-foreign-minister-to-end-iran-sanctions.html

"Gandom Beryan in Lut Desert - hottest place on Earth," Wondermondo.com. http://www.wondermondo.com/Countries/As/Iran/Kerman/GandomBeryan.htm

Gluck. Jay and Sumi Hiramoto, editors. *A Survey of Persian Handicraft: A Pictorial Introduction to the Contemporary Folk Arts and Art Crafts of Modern Iran*. Tehran: Survey of Persian Art, The Bank Melli Iran, 1977.

Habenstein, Robert W. and William M. Lamers. *Funeral Customs the World Over*. Milwaukee, WI: Bulfin Printers, 1960.

Hourani Albert. *A History of the Arab Peoples*. New York: Warner Books, 1991.

Howard, Jane. *Inside Iran: Women's Lives*. Washington, DC: Mage Publishers, 2002.

"Iran: The Essential Guide to a Country on the Brink." *Encyclopedia Britannica*. Hoboken, NJ: John Wiley and Sons, 2006.

Mackey, Sandra. *The Iranians: Persia, Islam and the Soul of a Nation*. New York: Dutton, 1996.

Maghazei, Malihe. "Iran," *Teen Life in the Middle East*, edited by Ali Akbar Mahdi. Westport, CT: Greenwood Press, 2003, pp. 13–31.

Momen, Moojan. *An Introduction to Shi'a Islam*. New Haven, CT: Yale University Press, 1985.

Nasr, Val. *The Shia Revival*. New York: Norton, 2006.

Price, Massoume. "Ramadan in Iran," Culture of Iran, http://www.cultureofiran.com/ramadan.html

Sharma, Amol Krishna Pokharel, and Gao Sen, "Ancient Sport of India Touts Ties To Buddha, and Male Cheerleaders," *Wall Street Journal*, Eastern Edition, August 26, 2010, p. A1.

Shackle, Samira, "Persian Facts." *New Statesman*, Vol. 141, Issue 5109, (June 11, 2012), pp. 24–41.

Waines, David. *An Introduction to Islam*. New York: Cambridge University Press, 1995.

Wright, Robin. *Dreams and Shadows: The Future of the Middle East*. New York: Penguin Press, 2008.

Wulff, H. E., "The Qanats of Iran," *Scientific American*, Vol. 218, No. 4 (April 1968), p. 94.

GLOSSARY

ayatollah (eye-uh-TOE-luh)—A high-ranking Muslim cleric.

caviar (CAA-vee-ahr)—The eggs of fish, mainly the sturgeon, that are regarded as a delicacy and eaten by many people.

chador (chah-DOOR)—A loose-fitting robe that covers every part of the body except the face.

clerics (CLAIR-iks)—Religious leaders.

dynasty (DIE-nuss-tee)—A line of rulers from the same family.

hijab (HEE-job)—A head covering worn by Muslim women and girls in public.

imam (ee-MAWM)—The prayer leader in a modern Islamic mosque; also one of 12 historic Shiite Muslim religious leaders.

manteau (man-TOE)—A knee-length or longer coat worn by many Iranian women instead of a chador.

martyr (MAR-tuhr)—Someone who willingly gives his or her life for his or her country or religion.

monarchy (MAHN-ar-kee)—A government under the control of a king.

provinces (PRAW-vihn-suhs)—Administrative divisions of a country.

sanctions (SANK-shuns)—Penalties imposed by countries on one another by hurting their economies, often by blocking imports and exports.

shah (SHAW)—A Persian word meaning king.

tectonic (tek-TAHN-ik)—Referring to plates or shelves of rock that move against one another beneath the surface of the earth, causing earthquakes.

theocracy (thee-AW-kruh-see)—A government based on religion and run by religious leaders.

INDEX

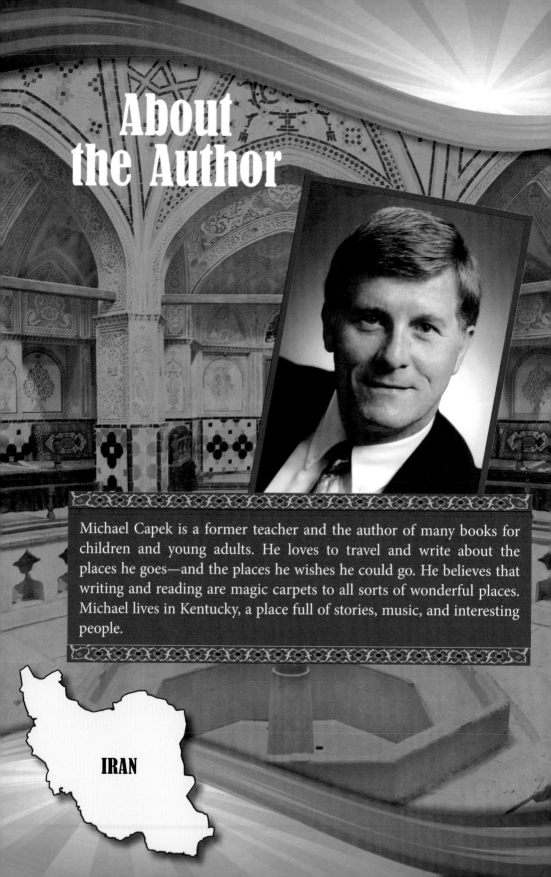

About the Author

Michael Capek is a former teacher and the author of many books for children and young adults. He loves to travel and write about the places he goes—and the places he wishes he could go. He believes that writing and reading are magic carpets to all sorts of wonderful places. Michael lives in Kentucky, a place full of stories, music, and interesting people.

IRAN